The Yoredale Way

By the same author:
THE EBOR WAY

The Yoredale Way

A 100 mile walk from York to
Kirkby Stephen

by
J. K. E. Piggin

Dalesman Books
1980

The Dalesman Publishing Company Ltd.,
Clapham (via Lancaster), North Yorkshire

First published 1980

© J. K. E. Piggin 1980

ISBN: 0 85206 592 2

Printed by Galava Printing Company Limited, Hallam Road, Nelson, Lancashire

Contents

The cover photograph, looking north across Wensleydale near Aysgarth, is by Geoffrey N. Wright.

Photographs in the text are on pages 25 - 32 and 49 - 56.

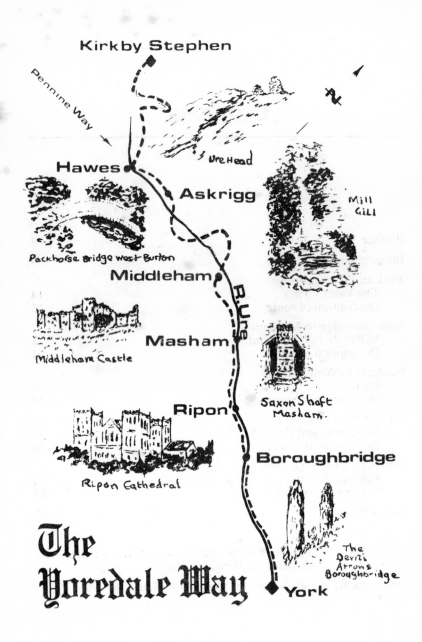

Kirkby Stephen

Pennine Way

Ure Head

Hawes

Askrigg

Mill Gill

Packhorse Bridge West Burton

Middleham

R. Ure

Masham

Middleham Castle

Saxon Shaft Masham.

Ripon

Boroughbridge

Ripon Cathedral

The
Yoredale Way

The Devil's Arrows Boroughbridge

York

Preface

One hundred miles in length—the Yoredale Way traces the River Ure from the point at which it joins the River Ouse, a few miles north of York, to its source 2,000 feet above sea level amongst the Pennine fells between Hawes and Kirkby Stephen.

Between these two points the walker along the Way will pass through the heart of Yorkshire, along delightful riverside paths, through undulating parkland and along ancient drove roads before achieving his or her objective amongst the grandeur of the Pennines. As the route is followed, visits can be made to many interesting towns and villages, ruined castles and the remains of a splendid abbey. While on the journey through Wensleydale, opportunities will be taken to divert into some of those wonderful tiny valleys through which the mountain streams pass and invariably produce impressive waterfalls before making their way to the River Ure.

This is a walk which will suit all tastes, the hardy long distance walker will no doubt accept the challenge and complete the walk in five days, maybe even four, but this should not deter the average walker. The paths are not difficult and the walk can be broken down into quite short distances and completed using cars and public transport. The exception is the Hawes to Kirkby Stephen section where public transport is only available at weekends from April to October when Dales Rail provides a very useful service which calls at Garsdale and Kirkby Stephen with bus connections to and from Hawes.

The route described in the following pages is only one of many, the main objective being to walk the length of the River Ure visiting places of interest along the way. Should you prefer to visit Bolton Castle instead of West Witton and wish to avoid the climb up Pen Hill or call at those delightful villages on the south side of the valley, by all means do so; there are adequate public footpaths available and no doubt you will derive a great deal of pleasure in planning a section of the walk yourself.

Badges, Completion Certificates and details of accommodation along the route are available from the author. Please send a stamped addressed envelope if you require information. Should anyone along the Way have accommodation available, particularly bed, breakfast and evening meal, I shall be pleased to hear from them.

First completed as a holiday 'jaunt' in 1977 and then by Tony Cronin, fellow member of the Ebor Acorn Rambling Club in 1978, the Way has subsequently been walked by the enthusiastic group who pioneered the Ebor Way. I am deeply indebted to all of them for their help and encouragement, particularly Tony who always manages to achieve his objective despite being provided with nothing more than an untidy handwritten manuscript.

During our adventures along the Way we met many wonderful and helpful people, many of them now our friends and thoroughly enjoyed ourselves in the process. Looking down over Lendal Bridge at the waters of the Ouse flowing below, we shall remember our walk to the source of the River Ure with great pleasure and hope that somewhere along the route some of you are enjoying the walk as much as we did.

Ken Piggin,
95 Bishopthorpe Road,
York. YO2 1NX

Introduction

Two thousand feet above sea level on top of the desolate and boggy fells known as Ure Head or Sails, between Hawes and Kirkby Stephen, two tiny streams, only a few yards apart, begin their journey to the sea. The most northerly one, the River Eden, makes its way down through that awe-inspiring chasm known as Hell Gill, which marks the boundary between Yorkshire and Cumbria, before turning northward to Carlisle and the Solway Firth. The other dashes down through deep channels in the side of the fell before turning southward on a long journey through the lush green pastures of Wensleydale and the rich arable land of the Vale of York to join the Yorkshire Ouse on its way to the North Sea.

The earliest recorded name of this river appears to have been Earp, but over the years this has changed many times, references being found to Jor, Jore, Yeure and Yore, before it seems that the river finally became known as the Ure in the 15th century. Certainly this name had become established by the middle of the 16th century as Leland, that famous antiquarian and chaplain to King Henry VIII, referred to it by that name in his writings on Yorkshire.

Authors ever since seem to have preferred the more attractive Yore making frequent references to it by that name; a river which provides the setting for some of the finest and most varied scenery in England, all of it within the reach of anyone with a firm step, strong lungs and a good pair of boots.

Those who walk the Way will certainly appreciate the topography of the hills in Wensleydale which resemble giant staircases on which the inhabitants of Yoredale established their drove roads and on which present day walkers will find that they provide an opportunity to have a rest and view the magnificent scenery before making the next climb. The outline of this hill formation is best viewed looking westward into the valley from the Jervaulx and Middleham area and is formed by alternate layers of soft mudstones and much harder sandstone and limestone many hundreds of feet in thickness. This structure was also responsible for the many fine waterfalls in the area, the Yoredale Series as it is called, and was detailed by one of England's most illustrious geologists,

John Phillips who was involved in the great geological survey of the British Isles. In addition he was author of many books and papers on the subject including **Illustrations of the geology of Yorkshire** and became the first curator of the museum at York, the starting point for this walk. John Phillips was buried in York cemetery. He died as a result of a fall from a much more modern staircase, that of All Souls College, Oxford.

For almost half its length the Yoredale Way passes through the Yorkshire Dales National Park, entering at West Witton and continuing to the northern boundary at Hell Gill. The National Parks were established in order to promote the enjoyment of certain areas of the countryside by the public for quiet recreation and to preserve and enhance the natural beauty of the area. In the Dales National Park Department the walker will find an enthusiastic band of people dedicated to these aims, often torn between the need to encourage enjoyment of the countryside, the preservation of the natural beauty and the necessity to maintain an environment in which the dales folk can continue their activities without hindrance. Walkers along the Way are asked to help them in this difficult task, not just by adherence to the Country Code, but by active participation in the furtherance of these aims. Please remember almost all land in the National Park remains in private ownership; respect other people's property as if it were your own. Report broken walls or fences, stray cattle and the like, pick up any plastic bags, glass, tins or other litter, and keep to the footpath at all times and above all do not climb walls. The structure of a drystone wall is such that removal or even displacement of the topstones can cause the collapse of the entire wall due to the penetration of frost and moisture. Should you see anything which you think warrants the attention of the National Park Warden, report it to the Information Centre at Hawes or Aysgarth Falls, or the National Park Office at Bainbridge or Grassington.

Long sections of the Yoredale Way pass through grassland where cattle are likely to be grazing, please make sure that all gates are shut and those pieces of wood or other material which cover stiles are replaced. They are put there to prevent the tiny lambs squeezing through the opening and becoming separated from the flock, not to inconvenience walkers. Sheep farming is one of the most important aspects of life in the Dales and it is requested that dogs should be kept on a lead at all times. During the lambing season the sheep will become restless even if they only scent the dog with possible serious harm to lambs or sheep resulting, so please during this hectic period, leave the dog at home. Dog owners should note particularly that dogs are forbidden at any time on Abbotside Common beyond Hawes. Please keep to single file across meadowland, especially in late spring and early summer, to avoid damage to the hay crop which is so vital for the economy of the hillfarmer.

The description of the route has been divided into five sections each of which can be described as a good day's walk for a hardy long distance walker. The majority of walkers will, however, prefer to do the walk in much shorter sections over a longer period of time; visiting places of interest, having a chat with the local people, a pint of ale in the village inn or even perhaps meandering off the route to visit other places of interest. To assist walkers in organising their schedules to suit their own requirements a map has been included which indicates available public transport, Youth Hostels and other information. In addition a list providing details of accommodation, together with any information regarding path diversions is available from the author on receipt of a stamped addressed envelope.

For those about to set out on the walk, a reminder, make sure you are well equipped at all times, good strong boots are essential on all the sections and waterproofs, compass, whistle and first aid kit should always be carried. When climbing Pen Hill or any of the fells beyond Hawes remember that these are lonely places with little shelter available, always take spare warm clothing and if the weather takes a turn for the worse, get down off the hills at the first opportunity. A final word of warning; the area between York and Linton is subject to flooding, so if the Ouse is over its banks at York, walkers are advised to take a bus to Linton and join the Way in Linton Woods Lane or walk along the A19 to Shipton and then along the road signposted to Linton.

Finding the way.

It is hoped that before this book is published, waymarking in accordance with the Countryside Commission's recommendation (a yellow arrow for footpaths and a blue arrow for bridleways) will have been provided at points where difficulty is likely to arise. Whilst the directions provided in this guide are as accurate as possible at the time of going to print, it will be appreciated that changes are made from time to time, hedges or even walls disappear, buildings are demolished and woods felled. Consequently it would be most unwise to attempt the walk armed only with this guide. Invest in a set of 1:50000 Ordnance Survey maps, read the directions given in the book, mark the route on the map before setting out and use the map on the walk, referring to the book when problems arise or you have a few minutes to spare to refresh your memory.

Essential maps

1:50000	Sheet	91	Appleby
	Sheet	98	Wensleydale and Wharfedale
	Sheet	99	Northallerton and Ripon
	Sheet	105	York

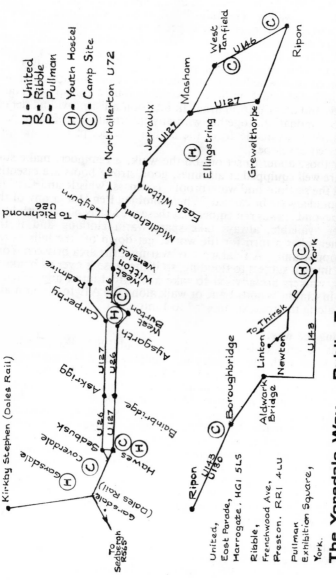

The Yoredale Way – Public Transport, Youth Hostels & Camp Sites

U = United
R = Ribble
P = Pullman
Ⓗ = Youth Hostel
Ⓒ = Camp Site

Kirkby Stephen (Dales Rail)

To Sedbergh RS65

Garsdale (Dales Rail)

Ⓘ Garsdale

Coverdale Ⓒ

Sedbusk

Hawes Ⓒ Ⓘ

U26

U127

Bainbridge

Askrigg

U26

U127

Carperby

Redmire

U26

West Witton

Aysgarth

Ⓗ West Burton Ⓒ

U26

Wensley

Witton

Middleham

Leyburn

To Richmond U26

East Witton

Jervaulx

U127

Ellingstring Ⓗ

Masham

U127

Grewelthorpe

U146

West Tanfield

Ⓒ

Ripon

Ⓒ Ripon

To Northallerton U72

Boroughbridge Ⓒ

To Thirsk

Linton
Newton

Aldwark Bridge

P

U143

Ripon

U143
U130

York Ⓗ Ⓒ

United,
East Parade,
Harrogate., HG1 5LS

Ribble,
Frenchwood Ave,
Preston. RR1 4LU

Pullman
Exhibition Square,
York.

12

The following 1:25000 maps are not really essential for those walkers who intend to keep to the route described, the list is provided primarily for the benefit of those who wish to explore the area away from the route described or devise their own deviations from it.

NY 70	Kirkby Stephen	SE 19	Catterick Camp
SD 79	Baugh Fell	SE 27	West Tanfield
SD 89	Thwaite	SE 28	Bedale
SD 99	Askrigg	SE 36	Boroughbridge
SD 98	Stalling Busk	SE 37	Ripon
SE 08	West Witton	SE 46	Tholthorpe
SE 09	Reeth	SE 45/55	York West
SE 18	Middleham		

The Country Code

All those who walk in the countryside are asked to observe the Country Code:

Guard against all risk of fire.

Fasten all gates.

Keep dogs under proper control.

Keep to the paths across farm land.

Avoid damaging fences, hedges and walls.

Leave no litter-take it home.

Safeguard water supplies.

Protect wild life, wild plants and trees.

Go carefully on country roads.

Respect the life of the countryside.

York to Boroughbridge

THE VALE OF YORK

'Come spur away, I have no patience for a longer stay
But must go down and leave the changeable noise of this great town
I must the country see.'
—Thomas Randolph

A look at the map will reveal little special between York and
Boroughbridge, the Vale of York stretches out to right and left and
our walk takes us along quiet riverside paths for most of the way.
If one looks a little closer however, it will be seen that this stretch
of the river is unique in that four of Yorkshire's rivers; the Ure,
Swale, Nidd and Ouse all join forces between York and Myton-on-
Swale. The Ure joins the Ouse at a point just north of Linton Locks
where a tiny stream called the Ouse Burn trickles into the river, the
point being marked by a sign on the western bank. Unfortunately
this stretch of riverside path is not a public right of way and for
the present the Way will join the Ure at Aldwark and then again
beyond Myton, although it is hoped to obtain permission to use
the riverside path eventually.

There is however much of interest along the path, in fact before
leaving York there is the imposing Gothic architecture of St.
Peter's school across the river on the northern bank. It is the
second oldest school in England and its history goes back to
627 A.D. The school's most notorious scholar was of course Guy
Fawkes who was born in the shadow of York Minster.

Just beyond the tiny village of Beningbrough is Beningbrough
Hall standing among delightful woodland which stretches down to
the river's edge. It is a fine building, the present Hall was built in
1716 and replaced the original structure which stood some three
hundred yards to the south east. Famous for some magnificent
carving, the house is now owned by the National Trust who have
produced a guide which describes the rooms which are open to the
public and tells the stories of some of the inhabitants of the past.

The next point of interest can be seen quite clearly as the path
leaves the woodland surrounding the Hall, for the tall spire of All

Saints, Newton is an impressive 150 feet high and can be seen from Brimham Rocks in Nidderdale. In the church are magnificent brass portraits of Viscount Downe and his wife, he in clerical robes with two lions at his feet and she with her feet on a cushion and a dog beside her. The fine old stone lychgate originally stood nearer and parallel to the church. In the nineteenth century Newton Feast was held on the Tuesday and Wednesday of Whitsuntide week when entertainment was provided by the Newton Brass Band and a barrel organ provided music for dancing on the village green. The present day's feasting takes place at the **Dawnay Arms** where walkers are made very welcome.

One mile from Newton are Linton Locks, constructed in the latter part of the eighteenth century, they flourished until the Linton Lock Company collapsed in 1920. A small hydro-electric power station was built in 1923 to supply York with electricity, but this became uneconomic and closed in 1961. A period followed when the locks fell into disrepair, but they were eventually rescued and utilised by the present marina and caravan park. The village of Linton possesses little of interest so far as buildings are concerned, but it is of course famous for its airfield which was the base for the Halifax, Whitley and Lancaster bombers during the Second World War.

Aldwark, the next village on the Way, has a church at one end and a pub at the other, the church dedicated to St. Stephen was built in 1846-53 and is of very interesting construction, since it was built with a mixture of local field stone and courses of herring-bone brickwork.

Just beyond the tiny village of Myton the path crosses a meadow where the Swale and Ure meet. In 1319 this was the place where the English were defeated by the Scots in the battle known as the Chapter of Myton or the White Battle, so named because a multitude of York clergy fought in the battle dressed in their surplices.

Boroughbridge, which has plenty of accommodation and bus services to York and Ripon, is an excellent place to finish this section of the walk. Once a very prosperous town standing on the Great North Road, in the middle of the nineteenth century it was a busy port having a regular service of vessels carrying materials and produce to Hull. The town was the setting for Barnaby Fair which lasted for ten to fifteen days and was an annual holiday for all the people in the surrounding countryside. A very old charter ordained that anyone could sell ale without a licence on Great and Little Fair days, providing that they hung a bush in front of their house which was appropriately called a Bush House. The Devil's Arrows just outside the town and on the next section of the walk are pillars of millstone grit each eighteen to twenty feet high and weighing twenty six to thirty six tons. They are thought to have been carried

15

from Plumpton during the Ice Age to be erected eventually by Neolithic man, but for what purpose has never been discovered. In an adjoining field known as Arrows Close, a large quantity of shaped flints were found.

Not actually on the walk, but only a short distance from Boroughbridge is Aldborough, the site of an ancient Romano-British city which is well worth a visit. Here stood the city of Isuer, capital of the Brigantes, later to become the Isuerium of the Romans. About the end of the first century it was plundered by the Engle folk and then again by the invading hordes from Scotland after their victory at Myton. The museum at the south entrance contains many relics found in the city. The church built in 1360 has an interesting Roman altar against the West wall. The register recalls the plague at Boroughbridge in 1604 during which some eighty people died.

YORK TO BOROUGHBRIDGE
(20 miles)

Start the walk at the gates of York's Museum Gardens where there is an immediate choice of routes, either make your way down the slope to the river or cross Lendal Bridge and take the path on the other side. It is really only a question of personal preference for both are attractive walks. For my part, I prefer the south bank with its splendid view of St. Peter's School across the waters of the Ouse. Assuming you have chosen likewise, go as if to walk along the Bar Walls and turn right down some steps to the riverside, turning left past the York City Rowing Club boathouse and walk along the river bank to the railway bridge. Go under this bridge, which carries the York to Scarborough line, and continue along the river bank on the grassy tree-lined path to Clifton Bridge, turning right across the river, but staying on the same side of the road. Incidentally for those staying at the Youth Hostel, this will no doubt be the starting point for the Youth Hostel is hidden amongst the trees on the left after crossing the bridge. It is also the point at which we shall meet our friends who have chosen to take the path along the northern bank of the river.

The path now continues down the slope, under the bridge and along the northern bank where one can either take the rather muddy path along the river's edge or the high level one which will keep your feet dry. Where the bushes along the edge of the bank end is Clifton Ings and once again there is an alternative, you can either take the path along the bank or the other one which goes to the right, cutting off the wide sweep of the river.

From this point to the village of Beningbrough, there is little need for a detailed description as the path continues along the river's edge all the way—approximately nine miles of pleasant

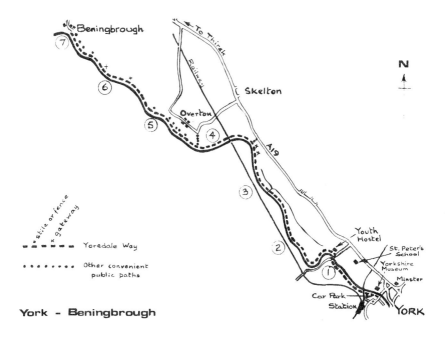

York - Beningbrough

walking, while the slow flowing Ouse, disturbed only by the occasional motor boat gives little indication of the many changes which will take place on the journey to the high fells where the walk will end.

After the long stretch across Clifton Ings, the path continues along the riverside, then through a small wood, past a bungalow and finally on to the point where the railway to Scotland passes over the river. Just after the bridge you will see the village of Poppleton on the opposite bank. After nearly three more miles, the tiny village of Beningbrough is reached where unfortunately there isn't even a shop.

From Beningbrough to Newton is a delightful stretch of the river, particularly at Nun Monkton, but there is no bridge where the River Nidd joins the Ouse, and on our side of the bank Beningbrough Hall stands majestically in its parkland. The riverside walk continues over stiles and along a wonderful tree-lined path to Newton, a place easily recognized by the church spire towering above the village. As you approach the village, the path cuts up to the right away from the river toward a bungalow where a stile provides access to the village street, the church and to a couple of pubs. For those who are more interested in a quick jug of ale than the attractions of the village, there is a path which continues along the river bank, behind the church and into the back garden

17

of the **Dawnay Arms.**

Sixty yards beyond the **Dawnay Arms** (should you have refreshed yourself there, turn left on leaving) go up a track on the right at a sharp corner in the road where you will find a public footpath sign beside a gate. Go through the gate and straight ahead to another one after which the path veers left toward the River Kyle and to a stile almost at the river's edge. The path now continues a little way from the river on the higher and much drier ground for approximately a mile, at which point a farm can be seen over the river to the left. Look for a tiny hump-backed bridge constructed of brick which has seen better days, but yet is perfectly safe. Cross it, climb over a gate and go straight ahead through another gate and along a very pleasant green track which passes through the farmyard and onto Linton Woods Lane. Keep straight ahead along the lane, walking past farms on the right, as the track changes to a pleasant green lane which continues to the village of Youlton. Turn left and take to the quiet country road for one mile then, about a quarter of a mile past a farm on the left, turn right down a very clear track to the right, marked 'Private, Keep out'. Just beyond a solitary gate-post on the right and before a gorse bush on the left, veer left on a track between marshy ground and bracken. Next pass to the right of another large clump of gorse and go forward on what is now a green track leading to the boundary fence of the wood on the right. Continue alongside the fence, past some trees on the left to the end of the wood and to some open country beyond, where you will find the stump of an old tree. To the left is a clear path through the centre of the field and the spire of Aldwark church beyond. Go along this track, then through a couple of gates, turning right on the tractor track after the second one. Proceed through another gate and turn left out onto the road, lastly turning right into the village.

Walk on past the **Bay Horse** and continue straight ahead along a lane signposted 'Bridle Road'. This is a really splendid walk along a wide track with excellent views of the North Yorkshire Moors and the White Horse of Kilburn over to the right. At a sign which bars anglers from any further progress and also forbids them to fish after lighting up time, the track swings right and then left, then goes past a farm and along a tarmac lane to a minor road. Turn left along this road to the village of Myton, past the old church and the pump, which was given its protection in 1870, and on to the last house on the right. After this a track goes down to the right to a bridge over the River Swale.

Our contact with the Swale is but a fleeting one, for after crossing the bridge, we step over a stile, and take a diagonal path away from the river to a point where a hedge meets a wood. This meadow incidentally is the place where the White Battle was fought so you will be able to survey the battlefield fully as you take the

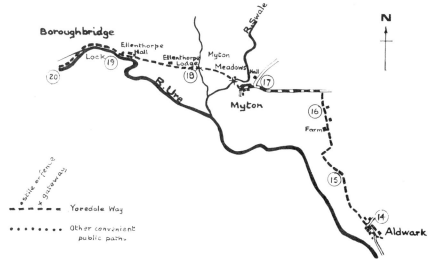

Aldwark – Boroughbridge

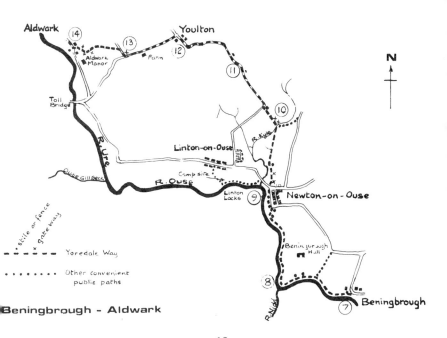

Beningbrough – Aldwark

longest path across it! If you have judged things right, you will find amongst the trees a bridge over a stream and straight ahead a track with a hedge on the right which leads to Ellenthorpe Lodge. At the farm go straight ahead and through the farm buildings, turning right and then left, then pass a cottage on the left and walk along the access road all the way to Ellenthorpe Hall which can be seen straight ahead.

Just before the farm buildings at the Hall, cut down to the left and through a small gate and turn right along a path which passes along the river's edge in front of the Hall. The path now follows the river all the way into Boroughbridge. Minor obstacles in the shape of a little barbed wire and bank erosion make things a little uncomfortable at the end of a long and tiring day, but these things are quickly forgotten when the locks are crossed and the Way continues along a very pleasant tree-lined grassy track into the town. Boroughbridge, a halting place in days gone by, is certainly a very good place to rest your weary bones and build up your strength for the next section.

Boroughbridge to Masham

**'By falling stream and standing hill,
By chiming tower and whispering tree'.**

—A. E. Houseman

The twenty miles between Boroughbridge and Masham can hardly be described as well-known walkers' country and yet it contains some of the finest and most varied riverside walks in Yorkshire. Our route takes us along pleasant walks beside a placid, slow flowing river, a canal towpath and finally the magnificent path through Hackfall woods where the river snakes its way through a deep gorge; a complete contrast to the early part of the walk. In addition there is a stately home, a cathedral, many interesting churches, delightful villages and last but not least, quite a few establishments where walkers are welcome and which in most cases provide a first class snack as well as the usual liquid refreshment. What better ingredients for a most enjoyable day out in the country?

Passing the Devil's Arrows on our way out of Boroughbridge, we soon arrive at Roecliffe, always clean and well kept, as the gardens are full of bloom in spring and summer and the green is always trim and inviting. The church possesses a collection of very old church furnishings which have been discarded by other churches.

About three miles from Roecliffe there is a fine view of Newby Hall, a magnificent house built in 1705 from designs by Sir Christopher Wren. It was at this point that a disastrous hunting accident occurred on February 4th 1869 when a fox chased by the hunt crossed the river to be followed by Sir Charles Slingsby and several members of the hunt in the ferry boat. On the way across one of the horses jumped out of the boat and became entangled in the chains turning the boat over, Sir Charles and several members of the hunt being drowned.

Ox Close Locks a little further along the river marks the beginning of the Ripon Canal which in the days before the advent of the railway carried a great deal of materials and produce into and out of Ripon. Bought by the railway company, the canal was allowed to deteriorate beyond repair and is now used as a mooring place for the motor boats. For those more interested in horses than boats, the racecourse lies between the canal and the Ure.

Space and indeed my meagre knowledge of the history of Ripon and its Cathedral limits the contribution in this book, but those who desire to know more will find that most of the books on Yorkshire include chapters on the city and its history. The Cathedral, a magnificent building which dominates the whole of the countryside around Ripon, was completed in its present form soon after the beginning of the sixteenth century. In the market square an obelisk 90 foot high forms the focal point and carries a plaque which tells the story of the town's Wakeman whose principal duty was to set watch at nine-o'-clock by blowing a horn, a custom which has survived to the present day. There is of course much more to tell of the Wakeman and his duties, but this is best learnt at first hand by attending the horn blowing ceremony. The ancient chapel of St. Mary Magdalene which is on the Way between the Cathedral and the river bridge is also very interesting. Attached to the chapel in days gone by was a hospital for the poor and those afflicted with leprosy. In later years it was used as a hospice for strangers, clergy and wayfarers who came to Ripon. The present day wayfarer will find hospitality on the other side of the road!

But we must leave Ripon and continue on our way through that delightful area of parkland, woods and ponds which attract the naturalists and bird watchers. The area is owned by the Ministry of Defence and used for army training purposes, so walkers are requested to keep to the paths.

Our route continues through the village of North Stainley and we trace our way round the grounds of Slenningford Grange, then along the attractive riverside walk through the caravan and camp site at the mill and on to West Tanfield.

Tanfield is one of those charming places which are so popular with artists and photographers, the church and Marmion Tower providing an impressive background for the river flowing through wooded banks and under the old stone bridge. In the church are monuments to the Marmions, those celebrated knights mentioned in Sir Walter Scott's **Chronicle.** There is also a very interesting cell which is only about four feet square and has a squint opening through which one can see the altar. In the churchyard is a tombstone which records the death of Francis Thompson of Binso who died in 1746 at the ripe old age of 111.

After a delightful stretch of the river with extensively wooded banks we arrive at Mickley, a most attractive village, a real picture in spring when the cherry trees which line the solitary village street are in full bloom. The entrance to Hackfall woods, one of the most impressive places on the Ure is a mere two hundred yards beyond the old mill and can best be described in the words of Edmund Bogg in his book **Beautiful Wensleydale:**

The lover of the sublime and picturesque will be delighted with the shady solitude of the solemn woods, hanging high o'er the river, through every opening of which delightful peeps are to be obtained; here and there are dark avenues which the light can scarcely pierce; now the path winds up some steep incline where a brook is gurgling out a song of wild delight, as it flashes and plunges down the shady dells, under beautiful arches composed of huge trees and dense foliage, the glittering sunshine the shadows of the leaves and branches on the path, like the images on some old cathedral aisle; or a huge rock stands boldly forth from the precipice above, bathed in the full glow of the sunlight, its riven form and weathered flanks adding to the river a sense of age and immobility. And so we wander; and the lovely, the majestic, the beautiful, the fascinating, still continue to increase until we reach Mowbray Point, just before sunset, and look over the thousands of green robed trees on to the winding river below, majestically flowing through a wondrous gorge. The enchanting views obtained from this standpoint are indeed marvellous.

From this vantage point one can see the magnificent octagonal spire of Masham church which marks the end of this section of the walk. The oldest thing in Masham is without doubt the lower part of an ancient cross which stands outside the church doorway; of Anglo-Saxon origin it is finely carved with the twelve apostles on the top and the adoration of the Magi on the lower portion. The churchyard also contains the remains of three famous local men, Julius Caesar Ibbetson a noted landscape painter in the eighteenth century, George Cuitt famous for his etchings of castles and abbeys who died in 1854 and lastly, William Jackson the musician who composed many anthems and settings for the Psalms. He was also quite a walker for he is reported as having walked to York Minster to hear an oratorio. Inside the church is a beautiful monument to Sir Marmaduke Wyville and his wife with their six sons and two daughters. The town is built round a spacious market square in the middle of which stands the shaft of the old market cross. In days gone by Masham cattle and sheep fair was said to be the largest in the country, upward of forty thousand sheep being brought to the fair. The town also has a brewery famous for its brew of 'Old Peculier', and inevitably several inns where food can be obtained.

Not on the Way, but only a short distance from Hackfall woods is the village of Grewelthorpe, at one time noted for the rich cream cheese which was made there. During the nineteenth century the villagers were employed in producing delightful walks through Hackfall woods which took visitors past a series of man-made ruins and rustic buildings, one of which can be seen along the Yoredale Way. For those who require more information about this charming place, there is an interesting history of the village entitled **Grewelthorpe - Now and Then** by Ann Williams which is on sale in local bookshops.

BOROUGHBRIDGE TO MASHAM
20 Miles

For those who are interested in the riverside scenery and the surrounding countryside, this section will provide many delights. The slow moving Ure at Boroughbridge gradually changes as Ripon is approached, Newby Park providing the first signs of change. Here the river passes through pleasant wooded parkland and one sees the first signs of the motor boats which dominate the river on this section up till Ripon, and the locks also provide interest as the boats negotiate them on their way along the river. Beyond Ripon one becomes aware of even more drastic change, the flat fields give way to rolling countryside, the river passes through deep gorges and the steep banks are heavily wooded, providing many wonderful views which only walkers can enjoy.

But I return to the route; after crossing the river bridge at Boroughbridge, keep straight on past the turning to the left, cross the road to the fish and chip shop and turn right up the lane just past the shop. The lane veers left and then right, past some bungalows, eventually turning left along a fenced track where in the field on the right the Devil's Arrows stand like sentinels guarding the crops. At the end of the track a gate leads out onto the road where another of the Arrows stands in a field at the opposite side, in a better position for close inspection. Turn right along the road, go under the bridge carrying the A1 and proceed for about 200 yards to a cottage called Willow Close, easily identified by the post box outside. Turn left along the track before the cottage which swings right, then left and then right again and crosses the old railway formation. At this point the red roofs of Roecliffe almost straight ahead can be seen. A word of warning, boots are essential along this track, as it is muddy even in dry weather, but really waterlogged when it rains. As you approach the village, the track swings right and out onto the road where a left turn and a couple of hundred yards of walking will bring you to this attractive place. For those who want refreshment, there is an excellent little shop and a little further into the village an inn where the landlord will be pleased to quench your thirst—providing you've arrived during licensing hours.

Alongside the churchyard there is a footpath sign which says 'Footpath to Westwick'; go through the kissing gate, alongside the churchyard wall, then step over a stile and veer left down the hill to

THE YOREDALE WAY

Since the Guide was written a few route changes and improvements have been made. The following brief notes should make the text a little less confusing and add to your enjoyment of the walk.

Aldwark — Leaving Youlton Lane go through the gate marked "Private — Keep Out" as in the text and then proceed straight ahead past a single gate post (Yoredale Way sign) and beyond it straight ahead to the right of a wood along a wide track. Turn left at the minor road into Aldwark and then right along the signposted Bridle Road to Myton. This is a path kindly agreed by Aldwark Estate and avoids crossing arable land. When walking in the reverse direction turn left at the public house in Aldwark and continue along the road to turn right along a wide track just beyond a cottage. Go straight ahead to Youlton Lane.

Ripon Parks — At North Parks Farm go through the gate about 50 yards before the farmhouse and straight ahead to join the wide track going to the left. Take care to turn along a track to the right as there is now a wide track which continues to the road.

Slenningford Grange — After swinging round the wood ignore the stile and continue straight ahead for 50 yards to turn left through a gate and up some steps going through an opening at the top and turning right to resume the path described. The route here is now well signposted in both directions.

West Tanfield — Go along the lane to Quarry House Farm ignoring the gate mentioned in the text and continue to a point just before the farm where there is a gate on the left (signposted Footpath to Mickley). Turn left through it and across the meadow to join the riverside path. The stile has now been blocked up and it is necessary to climb the fence. In the reverse direction go straight across the meadow towards the farm, passing through the gate to the right of it and then right along the track to West Tanfield.

Hackfall Woods - Nutwith Cote — At the end of Hackfall Woods go over the gate as in the text but turn right down a wide track which swings left alongside the river to join path described at Nutwith Cote. In the reverse direction keep straight ahead along riverside at Nutwith Cote, through a gate and along a wide track which eventually swings right and then left at top of hill to join route described at the gate leading into Hackfall woods.

Cover Bridge to Middleham — Additional stiles confuse the text. Continue along the bank of the Cover to a stone wall on the right where there is a stile hidden in the wall. Go through it and turn left to pass through another one and then right up a steep incline to turn left at the top. Go straight ahead to a stile and after passing over it veer right across the field aiming at a point midway between a black barn on the left and farm on the right to a stile hidden from sight by a dip in the field. Go over the stile and continue in the same direction to a gate and over the hill beyond to Middleham Castle.

Leyburn — Approaching Leyburn it is now necessary to pass through a new housing development but a clear path has been left alongside the houses and in approximately the same position as the previous path.

Pen Hill — After passing the farm on the minor road there is a right of way which is reached through a gate on the right just before a cattle grid and from there goes straight ahead to the summit of Pen Hill. Walkers using this path should be very careful to close the gate as cattle wandering out of this field can go only one way — downhill to a particularly dangerous stretch of road.

Aysgarth Falls - Bear Park — Bear right after passing Upper Falls up a hill and after passing through a gate turn right through the old railway formation and follow a waymarked route through the farm. Beyond a heavy wooden gate turn right through a stile and then left alongside a wall and along the waymarked route as described. In the reverse direction after passing through the last stile turn left through the heavy wooden gate and along waymarked route through farm to turn right into park, through old railway formation and left down to falls.

Wharton Castle - Kirkby Stephen — After the farm buildings at Wharton Castle go through the third gate on the right and climb hill to large boulder and continue in the same direction to a stile over the shoulder of the hill. Go over this stile, turn left over a step stile and along the riverside path described in the guide.

Two views of York, starting point of the Yoredale Way. Alternative routes out of the city follow opposite sides of the river Ouse from Lendal Bridge, seen in the lower photograph. (*Jack Wetherby*)

The village pond at Nun Monkton, close to the confluence of the river Ouse and Nidd. (*Robert Rixon*)

Boroughbridge, twenty miles along the Way, stood on the Great North Road until a by-pass was built in recent times. This study shows the old market cross. (*Jack Wetherby*)

The Yoredale Way leaves the riverside at Boroughbridge to pass the
Devil's Arrows, three pillars of millstone grit each some twenty
feet high which are thought to have been erected by Neolithic
man. (*Jack Wetherby*)

Newby Hall, a magnificent stately home built in 1705 from designs by Sir Christopher Wren. Walkers have a fine view of the building across the river. (*G. Bernard Wood*)

Bishop Monkton, a picturesque village close to the Ure between Boroughbridge and Ripon. (*Jack Wetherby*)

Ripon—Yorkshire's smallest city—is dominated by its cathedral. Apart from York, this is the most important settlement along the route of the Way. (*Jack Wetherby*)

West Tanfield, with the church and Marmion Tower providing an impressive background for the river flowing along wooded banks, is understandably popular with artists and photographers. (*Philip Sambrook*)

Above: The river Ure at Mickley, close to the entrance to Hackfall woods and one of the high-spots of the walk. (*Bertram Unne*)

Opposite, top: Walkers following the Yoredale Way through the woods near Mickley. (*Ken Piggin*)

Opposite, bottom: Park Square, Masham, a quiet corner of a town noted for its spacious market square and its brewery famous for 'Old Peculier'. (*David Joy*)

Kilgram bridge, between Masham and Middleham, is one of several ancient structures spanning the waters of the Ure. The Way passes Kilgram Grange, just visible in the background. (*J.P. Utley*)

Jervaulx Abbey, badly desecrated but providing a most complete ground plan, was founded during the 12th century by monks from Normandy. (*Ken Piggin*)

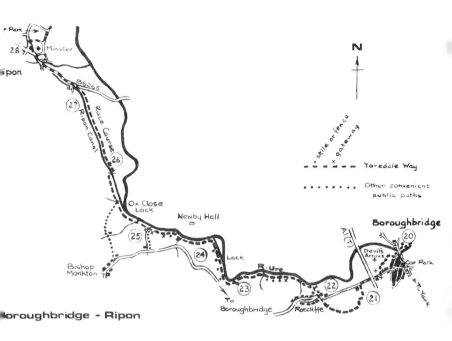

the river. Turn left along the river bank, the Ure is now broad and clear, as it gently curves its way through the meadows. This is a very pleasant walk, well-equipped with stiles and bridges except at a point where the track runs into a wood. Here it is necessary to negotiate a little barbed wire—care should be taken. The wood is an attractive place full of wild flowers in the spring and the path is easy to follow although a trifle boggy in places. As you emerge from the wood, lush green meadows can be seen ahead and the locks at Newby Hall come into view. Keep to the left bank at the locks and continue over stiles and through gates; the river is now usually lined with pleasure boats and presents a very busy scene on fine weekends. Should you hear the unmistakable whistle of a railway engine at this point, don't worry, it's not a ghost train, just the engine on the Newby Hall Miniature Railway and in a few moments you will see it puffing past the signal box on the opposite bank. A little further along is just the place for a five minute rest for there is a really magnificent view of Newby Hall with the terraced gardens leading down to the river.

Continue to follow the path which now goes through a wood and past a small marina, then along a tarmac track. Next go through a

West Tanfield

N

Slenningford
Mill Camp Site

34

Slenningford
Grange

33

North
Stainley

32

North
Parks

B6108

31

Middle
Parks

Ripon
Parks

Lakes

River Ure

North
Lees

South
Parks

30

stile or fence
x gateway

Yoredale Way

Other convenient
public paths

Camp
Site

29

Car Park

Minster

Ripon

Ripon - West Tanfield

34

gate and walk along the river bank to Ox Close Locks. At this point Ripon Cathedral can be seen ahead and it only remains for you to continue along the same side of the canal to a bridge, cross the bridge and go along the towpath at the other side of the canal into Ripon and a well deserved cup of tea.

If you intend to avoid the town centre, turn right at the roundabout, go past the cathedral and follow the caravan and camp site signs to the river bridge. Here you will see a footpath sign on the opposite side of the road which says 'Footpath to North Lees'. Go down the road called River View past the Sawmills, taking the track bearing very slightly right and go through a gate onto the riverside once again. Go carefully after this point for it is very easy to miss the path. Keep on the path nearest the river and continue until a wood comes down from the left and almost meets the path. Immediately ahead is a stile, do not go over it, just stand and look into the trees on your left where you will see hidden among them a footpath sign and a kissing gate. Scramble up the slope, go through the gate and into a meadow, turning right with a fence on the right. By this time you will have noticed a bungalow at about ten-o'-clock. Cut across the field towards it, passing through a gate and in front of it, then proceed through two more gates on the left and between the farm buildings. Keep straight ahead on the tarmac road to a junction where our track goes to the right through Ripon Park. This is a pleasant track with primroses and gorse bushes beside it but take care, as it is an army training centre. Keep to the track and do not touch unidentified objects. As you approach Middle Parks Farm, turn left through a gate, then go past a pond and swing right behind the farm buildings, next step over a cattle grid and walk straight ahead to another cattle grid. There is a track which goes left at this point but ignore it, continue straight ahead on the low track, under a power line and on to North Parks Farm. Past the farm go straight on through a gate between a cottage and an outbuilding, veering left across the field. Walk on through another gate and turn left along a good track which meanders slightly but eventually passes through a farmyard, past the cricket ground and into the village of North Stainley. If you require refreshment, turn left for the two inns are in that direction, otherwise turn right past the toilets and up a slight hill to a turning on the right just before the drive to Slenningford Grange. Go between a new bungalow and what appears to be a converted coach house on the right and just before an old house on the left called 'The Cottage', veer right down a tiny green path. Pass through a gate at the bottom of the hill, swinging left round the end of a copse for about fifty yards before turning left up a slight incline and over a stile hidden away in the hedge. Go up to a fence and turn right alongside it and over another stile about fifty yards ahead, passing over it and straight

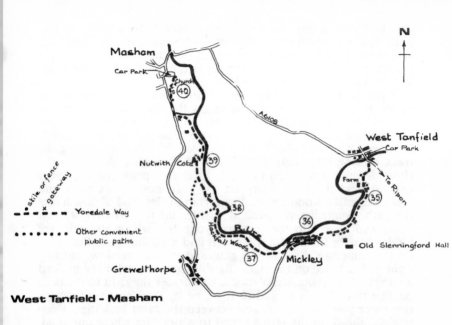

Masham

Car Park

Church

40

A6108

West Tanfield

Car Park

Nutwith Cote

39

Farm

To Ripon

35

38

36

stile or fence

x gateway

– · – · – · Yoredale Way

• • • • • • Other convenient
public paths

Hackfall Woods

R. Ure

Old Slenningford Hall

37

Mickley

Grewelthorpe

West Tanfield - Masham

ahead with a fence on the right to another stile. At this point you
will begin to appreciate the beauty of the district around West
Tanfield, the river down below making a delightful picture as it
wends its way through the bluebells to Slenningford Mill a few
hundred yards away.

A good track continues straight ahead into the caravan site. Go
past the site office as our path lies straight ahead, then on past the
old mill and along a beautiful stretch of the river to the bridge
at West Tanfield. This is a village which you will find difficult not
to linger in, for the church and Marmion tower are certainly worth
a visit and a couple of inns will provide you with any sustenance
you require.

On your return to the river bridge, follow the farm track on the
opposite side of the bridge signposted 'Footpath to Mickley' which
swings right past some pigsties and just afterwards there is a gate
on the left of the track. Beyond the gate is a fence, climb over
this and go along the edge of the field with a hedge on the left to a
wood at the opposite side of the field. Turn right along the side of
the wood and go through a small gate to join the river at a
point where, now much shallower, it makes a pretty picture
as it sweeps round a bend through tree-lined banks. Just beyond
this spot the path enters a wood, this can be reached either through
a stile and then by swinging right along the riverside or over some

wire netting and onto the same path. Whilst the former looks the more attractive proposition, those who choose it should be prepared to negotiate a rather difficult, and prickly, barrier of fallen trees and brambles. Continuing along the riverside, the path passes through the wood and a small gate and along a wide track in front of a large copper beech tree on the right. As the track swings left to Old Slenningford Farm, go straight ahead, cross over a stile and go through a small wood into a field with a wood on the right. Continue straight ahead to a gap in the wood, turning right over a stile beside a gate and walk across the meadow to the village of Mickley where a gate beside the end cottage on the right leads into a lane. Turn left along the lane and then right into the village street—a pretty sight in cherry blossom time. At this point it should be noted that the inn shown on most maps no longer exists so that you will have to wait for any drink until you get to Masham—but there are plenty of inns there.

Proceed to the end of the village, past the kennels on the left and the old mill on the right and climb up a steep hill to a left-hand bend where there is a footpath sign and a clear track going into the wood on the right. This is a really beautiful walk in good weather with delightful views of the river dashing through the gorge down below to the right and tiny streams rushing down from the tree-lined slopes to the left. The path is fairly easy to follow passing below a derelict building; the remains of one of those attractive rustic buildings built by the villagers of Grewelthorpe. Continue along the woods until a cart track goes up to the left beside a wood containing fir trees. Follow this track up the hill with a wall and wood on the right to a tubular gate near some gorse bushes. Turn right through the gate and continue parallel with the river keeping the wood on the right, immediately ahead you should now be able to see the tall spire of Masham church, no doubt a welcome sight if you have tackled this section in a day. Keep the fence on the right as you keep to the edge of the fields and turn right along a farm track to Nutwith Cote Farm where the path now goes to the right and down to the river's edge. Turn left along the riverside path, incidentally the river is now the River Burn, the Ure having branched off to the right just beyond Hackfall woods, and follow the path for about half a mile to a bridge. Turn right over the bridge and walk along the road for a quarter of a mile to a footpath sign with a stile beside it. As you cross the stile the path goes diagonally across the meadow to a black hut, passing to the left of it and across the next meadow to the church where a gate leads into the churchyard. Go through the churchyard to the main gate and the market square beyond.

Masham to West Witton

'Gone are the coloured princes, gone echo, gone laughter;
Drips the blank roof, and moss creeps after'.
— **Richard Hughes**

Leaving Masham our journey now takes us into Wensleydale, the largest of the Yorkshire valleys and an area which, during the Middle Ages, was the setting for intrigue and romance which helped to decide the fate of many of our kings and queens.

When you have passed through the tiny hamlet of Low Ellington, approximately half an hour's walk takes us to the beautiful ruins of Jervaulx Abbey set in delightful wooded surroundings. Desecrated to a greater extent than most other abbeys, the ivy clad ruins do, however, provide a more detailed ground plan of the monastery than any other. It originated during the twelfth century, founded by Peter de Quincey, a monk from Normandy. The abbey prospered for some four hundred years before its long peace came to an end with the Dissolution of the monasteries and the execution at Tyburn of Adam Sedbergh, the abbot, for taking part in the Pilgrimage of Grace.

Two miles onward and we arrive at Cover Bridge, for centuries a meeting place, firstly for warriors on their way to the wars, then for the more peaceful but still boisterous horse-dealers on their way to Middleham and now for the devotees of 'the gentle art', those patient individuals who fish the Ure and Cover. The famous inn will no doubt now get its quota of walkers for there are tasty snacks available plus of course the sort of welcome which one would expect at such a place. In September 1974 a thunderbolt caused extensive damage in the surrounding area, the electrical installation at Cover Bridge farm was put out of action, but the **Cover Bridge Inn** across the road suffered only one broken light bulb.

After a short walk along the tiny River Cover and a climb over the hill, we are rewarded by one of the best views to be obtained of Middleham Castle, a view which makes it easy to visualise the scenes of splendour across those fields when Warwick the King-maker 'entertained' King Edward IV. The castle was one of the strongest in the North, built toward the end of the twelfth century it replaced the pre-Norman fortress constructed of timber which stood on William's Hill, the mound south of the castle. After the death of the Earl of Warwick the castle passed into the possession of Richard III who had married Lady Anne Neville; their only son Edward was born here in 1473 dying 11 years later. The village contains two market crosses testifying to its importance as a market town, on one of which is a representation of a boar and which is known as the Boar or Swine Cross. The church is dedicated to Our Lady and St. Akelda who was reputedly martyred by the Danes for her fidelity to the Christian faith. There is a stained glass window in the church which depicts the saint being strangled by two females with a twisted piece of cloth. A holy well near which St. Akelda is supposed to have lived is in a field close by the church, the water being piped down the hill to the roadside where pilgrims would sit and bathe their eyes, the water being regarded as a cure for defective eyesight.

Across the valley lies Leyburn and whilst there is a much quicker way to get to the village of Wensley, anyone walking through Wensleydale would be missing a great deal if he or she were to take the direct path. Leyburn town is not in itself exceptionally pretty. It has a very large market place, certainly one of the largest in North Yorkshire, surrounded by the usual mixture of shops, inns and grey stone cottages which make it very much the same as any other town if it were not for the bracing air and magnificent views. We leave Leyburn on the famous Shawl where those views can be enjoyed to the full and pass by the spot known as 'Queen's Gap' where Mary Queen of Scots was recaptured after her escape from Bolton Castle.

Winding its way through the pretty parkland surrounding Bolton Hall, the route now continues to Wensley, the village which gives its name to the valley of the Ure. A charming place, Wensley was at one time the most important market town in the dale, but in 1563 a disastrous plague struck the village and, rapidly deserted by the inhabitants, it never recovered its former prestige. The church possesses some fine monuments, attractive carving and one of the finest brasses in England; a representation of a priest in eucharistic robes placed there in memory of Sir Simon de Wensley, a priest who lived in the reign of Richard III. The **Three Horse Shoes,** probably the oldest building in the village, got a mention from Drunken Barnaby with the following rhyme.

Thence to Wenchley valley seated
For antiquity repeated,
Sheep and Shepherd as one brother
Kindly drink to one another,

Till pot-hardy, light as feather
Sheep and Shepherd sleep together!

The path to West Witton lies along the south bank of the river, Pen Hill looming high over the village to the left and over the river, Bolton Hall can be seen standing majestically in the parkland. West Witton was a miner's village and late in the nineteenth century the narrow walled lane by which the village is approached was used by a procession of miners going to and from the mine across the valley. The church is dedicated to St. Bartholomew whose effigy is still burnt at the annual feast day in August, the ceremony being known as 'The Burning of Old Bartle'.

MASHAM TO WEST WITTON
(20 Miles)

Leaving the market place at Masham at the western end turn right and go down the road past the post office. Then take the right fork and continue down the hill to the river bridge. Just before the bridge turn left along the river bank at a footpath sign and proceed along a very pleasant three miles of riverside path to High Mains Farm. Approximately half a mile before Low Mains Farm the path skirts a wood and afterwards a gate cuts off a curve in the river with a wall and the outbuildings of Low Mains on the left. Yet another delightful little wood and the path emerges into a glade where across the river one can see Clifton Castle making a wonderful picture set amongst the rolling countryside; surely a place to stop and relax for a while for this is the end of the long walk along the river from Masham. Continue straight ahead for a short distance, keeping outside a wood and then sweeping left over to High Mains, one of the very few farms along the route where bed and breakfast can be obtained.

From High Mains take the track eastward veering right away from it before a cottage, then across to a gate and go through it on a good track which passes to the left of a hill. Leave the track just before the next gate, turning right to skirt the hill and onto another track which after half a mile emerges into the tiny village of Low Ellington at a stile which can be seen directly ahead. Turn right on entering the village, passing a farm on the right and keeping straight on until after the first field the track swings left and then goes straight ahead in a northerly direction to the river. This path is very easy to follow, since it is a short distance from the river most of the way, the occasional hillock providing a little variety and glimpses of the scenery in Wensleydale. At one point there is a splendid view of Pen Hill the end of this section of the walk. Walk through a couple of gates and our route continues straight ahead on a much wider track, over a stream and to the left of Kilgram

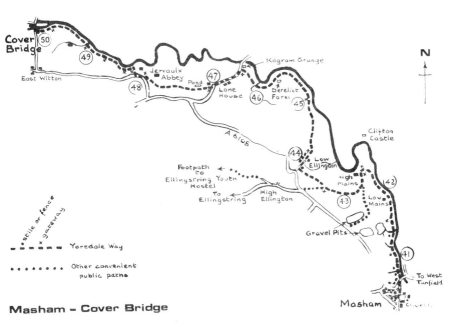

Masham – Cover Bridge

Grange. Go through a gate and onto a minor road. Turn left along the road for half a mile to the gatehouse at Jervaulx Park, turning right past the house and along a pleasant walk past a pond and through the parkland to Jervaulx Abbey. Next proceed past the abbey and go straight ahead to the A6108, turning right along the road for about three hundred yards where a track goes down to the right to the river. Turn left along the bank, the river is now much shallower than at Masham and the hills of Wensleydale seem to be much closer than they were at the other side of Jervaulx. After two miles of pleasant walking, the **Cover Bridge Inn** comes into sight, an appropriate place to celebrate for this is the half-way point of the walk. Over the bridge and just past the pub you will find a stile hidden away in the wall on the left, go through it and turn left along the edge of the field to the banks of the River Cover. Continue along the river bank and over two stiles until a gate bars the way. At this point take the path up to the right alongside the wood, turn left and go through a small gate. From the gate veer right between a farm on the right and a black barn on the left, then through another gate and continue in the same north westerly direction until at the top of the hill you will see Middleham Castle almost directly ahead. Aim slightly left of the castle and you will find a gate which leads into a lane which passes to the right of the castle and into Middleham.

41

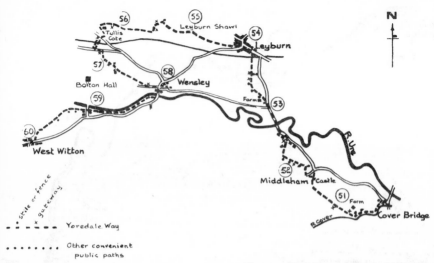

Cover Bridge – West Witton

You will no doubt wish to linger a while here for there is so much to see, but leave the old Swine Cross and church until last for the next section of the walk starts at the cross and passes through the churchyard. The cross is to the west of the castle and beyond it is a narrow lane which leads to a pair of stiles and a path into the churchyard. Turn left through the churchyard and go through a stile, across a field to another stile and past the end of a road to yet one more. Continue with the wall on the left through another stile and then turn right down the hill with a hedge on the right through yet another stile and past some bungalows on the right to a plot of spare ground. In the hedge you will find a tiny gate, go through it, across the plot, over a ladder stile and on to the Middleham to Leyburn road. Turn left along the road and over the suspension bridge which some writers have declared picturesque, some grotesque, for my part I would only say take great care and walk in single file for it is narrow and used by heavy traffic; a dangerous combination, particularly for pedestrians. At the road junction signposted Wensley 2 miles (please don't go down it, it may be a lot longer via Leyburn, but it is far more interesting and picturesque), go straight ahead and just beyond some farm buildings you will see a gate. Go through it and follow the track with the farm buildings on the left, past the farm and through a stile beside a gate. Turn right and cross through a series of three stiles heading straight for Leyburn church and a well-used path which goes over the railway bridge and into Leyburn. Turn left into the market place at the end of which is the **Bolton Arms** and to

42

the right of which is a lane signposted to Leyburn Shawl.

Go down the lane, turning left and then right through a kissing gate and along this splendid walk, enjoying for the first time a really good view of the southern side of the valley with Pen Hill, the end of this section of the walk, the dominating feature. It will be much better to ignore the view to the north as much as possible for over the wall is a stone quarry and you will be reminded of this by a notice which warns walkers not to go ahead when the siren sounds as blasting is about to take place. The path continues past Queen Mary's Gap and along the rocky ridge until approximately two miles from Leyburn and just beyond a gate with a stile beside it, a track goes down the hill to the left. Go down the hill to the remains of a wall and turn left across the field to a gate, passing through it and then turn right alongside a wood and straight ahead through two more gates to Tullis Cote Farm. Swing left after the farm buildings and along a very pleasant access road which winds down the hill to the Wensley to Preston under Scar road. Go through the gate on the opposite side of the road where there is a footpath sign, then across the meadow. Next proceed over the railway and another small field to a stile in the bottom right-hand corner and on to a minor road. Turn left along the road for a short distance and go down a wide track which goes into a wood on the right. Approximately eighty yards into the wood, turn left down a grassy track to a gate, go through it and across a field to another one. Turn right along another very clear track and through yet one more gate to a tiny cottage. Here turn left at the cottage and climb up towards the top of the hill with a concrete road, the main entrance to Bolton Hall, running parallel down below to the right. Veer right down the hill just before a wood to a gate, passing through it and on to the road, finally turning left along it and out of the main gates into Wensley village. If you are thirsty, then follow the path of **Drunken Barnaby** and turn left, but if you are more intent on completing the journey, turn right towards the church.

The last few miles of this section starts at a stile on the right just over the river bridge. The path, which is easy to follow passes through delightful woods occasionally opening out to provide splendid views of the river and the parkland of Bolton Hall on the opposite side. After about a mile the path swings up to a gate and along the side of the wood to a stile in the wall. Go across a narrow lane, and through three more stiles at which point Pen Hill looms over the village to the left and over to the right Bolton Hall can be seen standing majestically in its surrounding parkland. After the last stile, veer left up a small hill and follow the wall on the right to a stile which leads into a narrow walled lane and up the hill to the village. No doubt you have arrived feeling hungry and thirsty, well this is certainly the right place to be for there are three excellent inns which provide food and a welcome for walkers.

West Witton to Hawes

WATERFALLS AND DROVE ROADS

O'er my treetops, grave and brown
Slants the back of a breezy down
Through my fields by the covert edge
A swift stream splashes from ledge to ledge'.

—A. C. Benson

The next stage of the walk is completely different from its predecessors, for one thing we are suddenly confronted by a mountain, Pen Hill, which since ancient times has been one of a chain of beacon sites running the length and breadth of England. In May 1935 a beacon was lit here to celebrate the Silver Jubilee of King George V and Queen Mary and of course this was repeated in 1977 for the Silver Jubilee of Queen Elizabeth. Opposite across the valley is that great stretch of moorland which divides Wensleydale from its neighbour Swaledale.

From Pen Hill to West Burton we meet up with the first stretch of another feature of this section, the ancient walled tracks, the old drovers' roads, which in this case is thought to be the old Roman road between Middleham and the camp at Bainbridge; but which in later years saw a continuous stream of cattle passing along to Middleham Moor Fair.

Entering West Burton by the narrow packhorse bridge, one immediately appreciates this picturesque village standing in the shadow of Pen Hill where photographs taken now so closely resemble the sketches of the past. The Spire Cross stands at one end of the large village green, its crest a cock and at the base is a reminder of the past in the shape of the stocks where the local villains were punished. Down a narrow lane at the other end of the green is a pretty waterfall which is formed by Walden Beck rushing in a double cascade over a bed of shelving rock. This is the first and smallest of the three falls on this section of the walk. Waldendale from which lovely valley the beck flows was until the end of the nineteenth century the haunt of the red deer, and the wild cat and pine-marten were still to be found in the middle of that century.

It is only a short distance from West Burton to Aysgarth Falls, our route taking us through the churchyard of St. Andrews. The church contains some rich carving, particularly the elaborately carved rood screen which was reputedly brought from Jervaulx Abbey upon the shoulders of twenty men. Just beyond the church and beside the bridge is the old mill, built about one hundred and seventy years ago, it was originally a cotton mill but changed over to worsted to provide yarn for the local knitters and then when that industry died away, it operated as a corn mill. It is here that the River Ure, normally a placid slow moving river changes its character, falling in a broad curtain of three successive steps known as High, Middle and Lower Falls. They present a wonderful picture at any time, but to see them in all their glory one must visit them when the river is in flood and the water becomes a roaring torrent, the falls virtually disappear and the descent forms one great rapid, sending spray to the heavens. Up the hill is a car park, toilets, café and a National Park Information Centre. The Centre has an interpretive display of the Aysgarth area and carries local information and literature. It is open from March to November at weekends, and daily June to September (telephone Aysgarth 424).

Passing Nappa Hall, the home of the Metcalfe clan, that famous Dales family who fought with valour at Agincourt and Flodden, we arrive at Askrigg, until late in the 19th century a market town with two fairs per year, possessing three mills and noted for the fine clocks produced by its clockmakers. It was the first village in the dale and indeed one of the first in England to be lit by electricity, supplied from plant operated by the same stream which operated the mill wheels.

Between Askrigg and Hawes our route takes us over the old drove road which Mary Queen of Scots rode along on her way to imprisonment at Bolton Castle in 1568. Approximately one hundred years later in 1663, Lady Anne Clifford wrote in her diary of a journey along this road from Nappa Hall to her castle at Pendragon. This was the first time a four wheeled vehicle had passed along it and no doubt those of you who tramp along it to Pendragon will appreciate to the full what a hair-raising journey it must have been. There were in those days two villages along the track, Skellgill, now a tiny group of farm cottages, but which in the packhorse days was an important place with three inns, and Holehouse, one of the lost hamlets of Wensleydale which was situated just below Shaw Cote farm near the present road.

Hawes is at the end of this section and you will have passed through more than forty of those cunning little gaps in the walls which you no doubt called stiles at the beginning and something vastly different at the end. You will find this grey market town, nine hundred feet above sea level and at the very edge of the backbone of England, a hospitable place where walkers are accepted as part of the everyday scene for it is one of the main overnight stops along the Pennine Way. The chances are that you will be exchanging stories well into the night, but if you do have the time take a short walk past the lofty 19th century church and along the paved path to Gayle, a tiny village where the beck flows over innumerable rocky steps past the old mill and down into Hawes. The town is very well equipped to cater for the walker having several cafés and inns plus a few places where bed and breakfast can be obtained. There are toilets and the National Park Centre at the former station at the east of the town, with local information and an interpretation of the historic station and its goods yard. It is open weekends April to November, and daily June to September (tel. Hawes 450).

Thanks to the generosity of two of Wensleydale's most famous authors, Marie Hartley and Joan Ingilby, Hawes now possesses the Upper Dales Folk Museum, a remarkable collection of dales farming and domestic equipment which all who value the heritage of the Dales will wish to visit. Located in the old goods shed at Hawes station, the museum is open from Mondays to Saturdays 11 a.m. to 1 p.m. and 2 p.m. to 5 p.m. and on Sundays from 1 to 5 p.m.

WEST WITTON TO HAWES
(19 Miles)

Opposite the **Wensleydale Heifer** is a car park and a very pleasant little garden with a shelter in it—a convenient spot to don waterproofs if it is wet. Pass between the car park and garden and you will find a narrow snicket with a stile at the end of it which leads to a well-trodden path behind the village. After the second stile look towards the wood on the right and you will see, over the field, a stile in the wall. Go across the field, through the stile and turn right along a path through the wood which climbs slightly to a gate, pass through a stile to the left of it and then go straight ahead up the hill, now looking more like a mountain. Continue through stiles to the second of two walled lanes, ideal places to stop and admire the wonderful views and take a well-earned rest. At the second lane turn left for approximately two hundred yards and turn right through the second gate, climbing straight up to another gate and a third walled lane. Turn left along it to the road and then right up the hill, past a farm and continue to a point where the wall on the right ceases. Now turn right along a track over the moor and

Askrigg

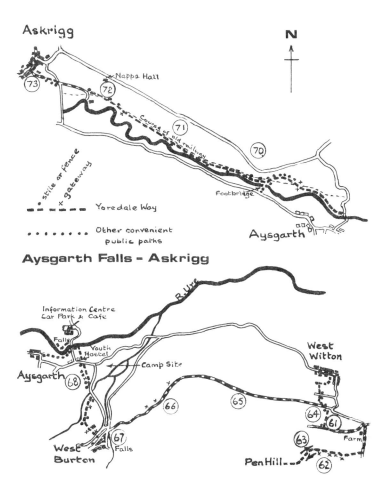

N

Nappa Hall

73

72

Course of old railway

71

70

Stile or Fence
+ gateway

Footbridge

Yoredale Way

Other convenient
public paths

Aysgarth

Aysgarth Falls - Askrigg

R Ure

Information Centre
Car Park & Cafe

Falls

Youth
Hostel

Camp Site

West
Witton

Aysgarth

68

66

65

64

61

West
Burton

67

Falls

63

Farm

Pen Hill

62

West Witton - Aysgarth Falls

after two hundred yards there is a small gate in the wall on the right, pass through it and then veer left on a path to another gate and then straight ahead through two more to the cairn beyond.

The walker will now appreciate why Pen Hill was one of a chain of beacons running the length and breadth of England for there are truly remarkable views from the top. The whole of Wensleydale spreads out below like a vast green carpet stretching from Jervaulx in the east to Hawes and our objective amongst the Pennines to the west.

There is a path which continues along the northern edge of the hill, but this is not a right of way. Walkers should retrace their steps down the hill to the second walled lane and turn left past the stile through which they passed on their way up. Continue along this pleasant green lane for about three miles of splendid walking and impressive scenery after which the track swings right and down a hill to the tiny packhorse bridge at West Burton.

There is really no need to go into the village for the footpath to Aysgarth Falls is reached through a tiny snicket located by turning left and then second right after the bridge and between some cottages on the right. It is, however, a charming place and besides it must be time for some well-earned refreshment. A pint of ale and a couple of Wensleydale sandwiches on the village green at West Burton in the shadow of Pen Hill is the ideal place to enjoy them. Before you do so however, it's worth a short walk along the road beside Walden Beck and through a tiny opening between the old mill and some cottages to the waterfall, the smallest but by no means the least pretty of the four you will encounter on the walk.

From the village pass through the snicket, across the road, go through a gate and straight ahead past a barn to Bishopdale Beck. At the beck turn right through a stile and then left to another stile, turning right away from the beck with a wall on the right, then through the football field to a stile. After passing through the stile, turn left along the road and over a bridge. Just after the bridge the road swings right and straight ahead there is an inviting walled track with a stile at the first bend, but ignore it for our path lies through a stile to the right of the gate just right of the track. Go through the stile and straight up the hill to another stile, once again just to the right of a gate. Through the stile cut across the corner of the field, go through yet one more stile after which the track runs almost due north through another two stiles and down into a small valley known as Thieves Gill. Proceed through a further stile, the path now goes straight ahead and continues up the other side of the valley and across a field to a stile. Cross the road for the lane leading to Aysgarth church. Go down the lane and through the churchyard, no doubt stopping to visit the church for it is well worth half an hour of your time, and continue through the churchyard and down to the bridge and one

Middleham Castle, once one of the strongest in the north, saw scenes of splendour when Warwick the Kingmaker 'entertained' King Edward IV. (*Bertram Unne*)

Leyburn Shawl provides—for the first time on the walk—superb views of the southern side of Wensleydale. (*Jack Wetherby*)

The bridge over the Ure at Wensley, a once important market town which gives its name to the river valley. (*Leonard & Marjorie Gayton*)

Walkers approaching West Burton by the old drovers' road from Middleham have a magnificent panorama up Wensleydale and across lower Bishopdale. (*Geoffrey N. Wright*)

Aysgarth Falls, best seen when the river is in flood and the water becomes a roaring torrent sending spray to the heavens. Early travellers favourably compared the falls with the cataracts of the Nile. (*Leonard & Marjorie Gayton*)

Above: Two backpackers tackle the stiff climb up the flanks of Great Shunner Fell from Hardrow. This path is common to the Pennine Way and the Yoredale Way. (*Geoffrey N. Wright*)

Opposite, top: The broad, green valley of Wensleydale as seen from Ellerkin above Askrigg. (*Geoffrey N. Wright*)

Opposite, bottom: The Tuesday market in Hawes, a town well equipped for walkers for it is one of the main overnight stops on the Pennine Way. (*Derek Widdicombe*)

Hell Gill, a deep limestone gorge which forms the boundary between
North Yorkshire and Cumbria, is only a mile from Ure Head.
(*Geoffrey N. Wright*)

Mallerstang as seen from a point close to the watershed separating the Ure from the Eden. High Abbotside and High Seat are on the right. (*Geoffrey N. Wright*)

Waterfoot, an attractive stretch of the upper Eden between the castles of Pendragon and Lammerside. (*Gordon Wood*)

St. Stephen's church at Kirkby Stephen, a Pennine market town which marks the end of the 100 mile trek from York. (*Derek Widdicombe*)

of Yorkshire's most picturesque places, Aysgarth Falls. Over the bridge and up the hill is the café and Information Centre, but our path lies through the gate just over the river bridge and along the well-trodden path beside the upper falls. The path cuts across a curve in the river, through a tiny wood and up onto the old railway formation. After a farm on the right, turn through a gate on the right and then turn left along the side of a wall and on through a series of four stiles. Count them carefully for after the fourth stile the path veers slightly left, through another stile and across the old railway formation to the river. Ignore the footbridge turning right over a stile and walk along the northern bank of the river and inevitably over more stiles. A little further along the path can be a little difficult to negotiate, particularly when the river is in flood, but this can be easily overcome by scrambling up onto the old railway track and down again a little further along. Pass a distinctive hill with a few trees on top known as Lady Hill and the path continues along the river's edge until at a point where the river swings away to the left, the path goes straight ahead and keeps close to the old railway. A quarter of a mile further along, go through a kissing gate on the right which is a little difficult to find in the hedgerow, and go up onto the old railway formation turning left along it. After a short distance there is a stile and the path continues along the northern boundary of the railway, through a stile and into a pleasant lane which leads to Nappa House. After half a mile, the lane joins a narrow road on the opposite side of which is a stile and the path now clearly defined continues through three more stiles and into a walled track. By this time you will have seen the grey stone houses of Askrigg directly ahead and it only remains to continue along the lane into the village where there are shops, a café and a couple of pubs.

On Askrigg churchyard wall is a sign pointing the way to Mill Gill and down the lane to the right of the church the path is clearly signposted past the old mill, over a tiny bridge and on to the waterfall; a pleasant secluded place popular with visitors.

On returning from the waterfall, instead of turning left to return to Askrigg, go straight ahead from the stile along a green track with a wall on the left which, after about half a mile, emerges into a narrow lane. Turn right along the lane passing some farms after about a mile and continue to the cottages at Skellgill. Here, after a narrow bridge, the track turns left and then peters out, our path continuing in the same direction, skirting round the hill you will have noticed as you approached the hamlet. As the track becomes clearer and swings westward, a farm and a clump of trees come into view and over to the left is Addlebrough, the hill on which the Romans settled during their occupation of the North. Past the farm the track is gated and continues straight ahead, skirting the northern tip of a plantation and on to join the access

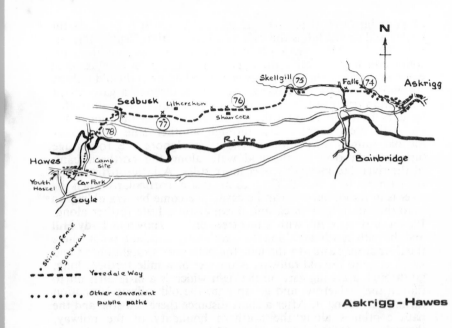

road to Litherskew Farm. This is a section of the walk where, with
little necessity to concentrate on route finding, one becomes aware
of the changing scenery. The valley is now much narrower.
the beauty of Upper Wensleydale more apparent and the Pennine
fells immediately ahead provide the first real indication of the
different terrain which will be encountered on the last section of
the walk. To return to our route, don't take the road up to the
farm, continue straight ahead, and go through a gate and along the
access road to the tiny hamlet of Sedbusk. The path misses this
small group of cottages and continues across the road and slightly
left. Go through a stile and then a further series of stiles, past a
farm on the left and through yet one more stile to a road. Go
through a stile on the other side of the road and continue in the
same south-westerly direction across a meadow, passing to the left
of a house and over to a wood where a tiny bridge over a stream
provides an excellent opportunity to have a rest before the final
stretch into Hawes. Carry on in the same direction to a stile and
after passing through it, turn left along the road, cross over the
river bridge, taking a short cut along a paved path into Hawes and
the end of this section.

Hawes to Kirkby Stephen

'Now I reach the mountain's brow
What a landscape far below;
No clouds no vapour intervene,
But the gay, the open scene,
Does the face of nature show,
In all the hues of heaven's bow'.

—John Dyer

The final section of the walk begins spectacularly at Hardrow where the Foss Beck takes a mighty leap of ninety feet into a rocky amphitheatre to form England's highest single fall of water. A third of the way up, a narrow ledge passes behind the falls giving the adventurous a chance to view this scene through the rushing curtain of water; an experience shared by Dorothy and William Wordsworth on their visit to Wensleydale in 1799.

Our journey now takes us up Great Shunner Fell, the start of twenty miles of walking through magnificent rugged Pennine country. A stiff climb up the fell, no doubt shoulder to shoulder with one of those hardy Pennine Way walkers and you will get your reward, wonderful views over the Buttertubs to Lovely Seat in the east and to the south-west Widdale Fell, Whernside and Ingleborough. Before we get to the top, however, we leave the Pennine Way and make our way down to the tiny and picturesque hamlet of Cotter. Here a group of cottages and farmsteads alongside the beck hurry down into Lower Cotterdale where three waterfalls make their way down through a thick curtain of ash, elm, rowan and hazel and provide a tiny paradise for artists and botanists.

But we must take to the high fells once again to follow the old drove road along Cotter End, the route used by the inhabitants of Cotter in days gone by to transport their dead to the church at Lunds and on to the High Way, an ancient road used by Lady Anne Clifford on her journeys to Pendragon Castle. Passing the Youth Hostel almost hidden away in the trees and having delicately forded quite a few streams dashing down to the valley below, we arrive at the point where the infant Ure also goes tumbling down the hillside. There is no designated right of way up to Ure Head and whilst there is a tradition of public access on the high fells and no objection is likely, walkers are reminded that this must be regarded as a privilege and not a right. A desolate and boggy climb is however, well rewarded by the splendid views and the satisfaction gained by reaching the source of three great rivers, the Ure and Swale to meet again at far away Myton and the Eden starting on its way to the Solway Firth. It is the latter that we join at Hell Gill, that terrifying chasm which marks the boundary between Yorkshire and Cumbria, for the remainder of our walk to Kirkby Stephen.

The Eden reserves its main delights for those who journey along it on foot as Wordsworth discovered and wrote of in his sonnet:

Eden! till now thy beauty had I viewed
By glimpses only, and confess with shame
That verse of mine, whate'er it's varying mood,
Repeats but once the sound of thy sweet name
Yet fetched from Paradise that honour came
Rightfully bourne, for Nature gave thee flowers
That have no rival among British bowers
And thy bold rocks are worthy of their fame.
Measuring thy course fair stream! at length I pay,
To my life's neighbour dues of neighbourhood;
But I have traced thee on thy winding way,
With pleasure sometimes by the thought restrained,
For things far off we toil, while many a good
Not sought, because too near, is never gained.

Along this delightful river we travel on to Pendragon Castle reputedly built by Uther Pendragon, a contemporary of King Arthur and one of the many castles owned by Anne Clifford Countess of Pembroke, Dorset and Montgomery who was by inheritance High Sheriff of Westmorland. The castle suffered extensive damage in 1695 when the Earl of Thanet used material from it to repair nearby Appleby Castle which was deemed to be of more importance.

A little further on are the remains of Lammerside Castle, a much smaller structure, of which little appears to have been recorded and beyond that Wharton Hall, a very impressive building which was at one time the Wharton family residence. The most famous member of the family was Philip, Duke of Wharton one of the cleverest men of his day who was reputed to hold orgies in the various Wharton residences in Westmorland.

Our walk through this section finishes as it began with a waterfall, not as spectacular by any means but very attractive and the ideal spot to rest awhile and remember all those interesting places you have visited on your long journey from York.

Another mile and you will arrive at Kirkby Stephen, the Pennine market town which marks the end of the long trek and where there are adequate cafés and inns to satisfy hungry and thirsty walkers. For those who fancy something more energetic than a pint of ale to celebrate the end of the walk, there is to the east of the town a splendid climb up Nine Standards Rigg, which was given its name by that intriguing group of cairns standing on the top 2,170 feet above sea level.

HAWES TO KIRKBY STEPHEN
(21 miles)

Leaving Hawes by the road signposted Hardrow beside the old station entrance, our route for the next few miles follows the Pennine Way. Over the river bridge and past the stile which marked the end of the last section, continue along the road for a short distance to the Pennine Way marker just beyond a wood on the left. Turn left through the stile and along the wood side on a clear track through stiles to Hardrow village where the entrance to the falls lies through the **Green Dragon**. Incidentally this is the only place between Hawes and Kirkby Stephen where refreshments are available and as you are unlikely to be there at opening time, make sure you have adequate food and drink for the journey before leaving Hawes.

Turn left along the village street, past the church on the right, over a bridge and along the road to a Pennine Way marker which indicates the route up a walled track on the right. This is a very stiff climb which taxes the muscles early in the morning, but there is an ideal spot for a rest at the gate where the walled track ends and where there is an excellent opportunity to look round and enjoy the scenery. Suddenly the countryside has changed and you are standing on the fringe of the Pennines, on the left is Mossdale Moor to the west of Hawes, over to the right is the famous Buttertubs Pass over to Swaledale and of far more immediate significance, the climb up Shunner Fell is directly ahead. The track is very easy to follow to the next gate, where the path turns to the left with a wall on the left after you have passed through it. After a short distance there are several cairns going off to the right marking the Pennine Way route, ignore them and continue straight ahead

61

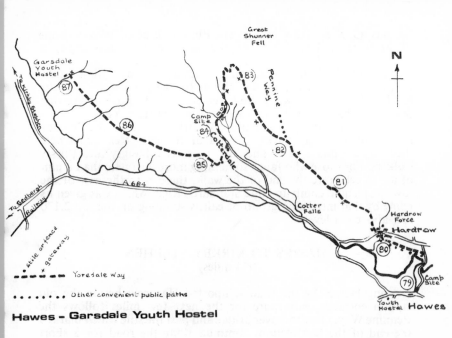

Hawes – Garsdale Youth Hostel

along the pleasant green track which has obviously escaped the thousands of feet which have continued on their weary way up the fell. The track skirts the western side of Shunner and soon you will see down in the valley to the left the tiny hamlet of Cotter and beyond the wooded slopes with a track winding up the hill, your next objective. Continue along the side of the fell, through a gate, after which the ground gets a little boggy and the track less obvious, with the forestry plantation on the left, until you see a gate on the left almost at the end of the plantation and certainly a long way past the point at which you would have expected to turn down into Cotterdale. Go through the gate and down the track into the valley and about half a mile from the cottages, you will find a track going down to the right past some small waterfalls to a bridge over the stream. Unless you feel adventurous and wish to ford the stream further down, go over the bridge and turn left along the stream into the hamlet.

After a delightful walk past cottages and farmsteads, the next stage starts about half a mile up the road where a wall goes up to the right at the edge of the forestry. Just before the cattle grid turn right over a fence and up the steep path between the forestry fence and wall. This is not a right of way, but a path used by kind permission of Mr. Metcalfe of Cotterdale. Continue up through a gap in the wall at the top and swing right to a small gate in a wall. Go through the gate and keep to the right of an old stone kiln, a very useful place to shelter when the weather is bad although you will find that the sheep have been there before you. The path continues with a wall on the left over which can be seen the Hawes to Sedbergh road down below in the valley. Continue at the same level, keeping that seemingly never-ending wall on the left for about three miles to Garsdale Youth Hostel which can quite easily be missed despite its close proximity to the track. Just beyond a stream there is an iron gate on the left and the Youth Hostel is to be found amongst the trees at the bottom of a waterfall. Alternatively it can be reached by continuing for about one hundred yards where there is a stile on the left and a path beyond which goes down to the hostel. By this time those non-members among you may well regret not having joined for this may well be your only chance to obtain much needed refreshment or a bed for the night.

Our path continues with the ever present wall on the left, along a clear track and fords three streams before the wall ends and we arrive at a fourth which passes through a small gorge on its way down into the valley. This is our real objective, the point at which the infant Ure dashes down into the floor of the valley below. Just to make sure that you are in the right place take a look around, about two hundred yards before this point the wall on the left should have ended and as you look ahead, you should see another wall which starts at the narrow gorge which has a few trees protruding from the rocks and trying desperately to survive. This then is the point at which you must decide if the long climb to Ure Head is worth the effort, but surely having explored the rest of this wonderful river it would be a pity not to trace this tiny stream to its source. Turn right and follow the stream up those deep channels gouged out of the fell side since the retreat of the ice more than ten thousand years ago. This is not a right of way, but the considerate walker is unlikely to meet any difficulty. About half way up the stream divides, do we go up left or right? The answer is quite simple, go up the middle and before very long you will see a cairn on top of the hill which is your objective. Having stumbled up the last couple of hundred yards, you will find that the cairn you saw is actually two separate cairns about ten feet apart, a splendid spot to celebrate the completion of this magnificent walk through Yoredale.

The top of Lunds Fell is not however, the place to end a walk, unless you have a friend who is a helicopter pilot, and I can think of no better way to finish this one than to make our way down alongside the River Eden, which also has its source up there on the fell, and follow it to Kirkby Stephen.

Standing at the cairn looking westward, you will see over to the right another cairn, make towards it, descending all the time and you will find yourself alongside the stream which dashes down the fell just like the Ure to turn northward to Carlisle. Keep to the southern bank of the stream and follow it down the fell to a bridge which spans a very deep gorge approximately half a mile further along the track which you left to follow the Ure. This is Hell Gill which marks the boundary between Yorkshire and Cumbria. Turn right over the bridge, go through a gate and along a green track which descends for approximately three miles to the valley below, providing the walker with some splendid views of Wild Boar Fell and along Mallerstang Edge. After a few boggy patches the track finishes at a gate through which our path continues to the right, along the road for a short distance, and through the first gate on the left. A track swings left and then right round a small hillock and over a bridge spanning the River Eden. Turning right along the river bank, you will soon find yourself with a wall stile to climb before proceeding along the bank to a farm. Go through the farm-yard, turning right along the access road and then left along the river bank before the bridge. Continue walking now through a pretty little wood to the good track to the cottages at Shoregill. The track passes round the back of the cottages and continues through a gate and into a walled lane for a short distance and then on through a small gate with a wall on the right. Climb over a stile and we can see our immediate objective, Pendragon Castle, straight ahead. It is now quite easy to find the way through a gate, over a small hill and over two more stiles, one of which appears to have been made from a railway signal ladder. Now cross a small stream and go through a gate beside the river bridge.

If you wish to visit Pendragon, turn right and cross the bridge, but to continue the walk, turn left past a cottage where the road swings right and up the hill to a cattle grid. Turn right along a well-defined track with a wall on the right, but which soon opens out to provide a real walkers' track. There is a mile of splendid walking along the valley with the impressive rocky outline of Mallerstang Edge over to the right and Wharton Fell to the left. Look for the power line crossing the track for two reasons, firstly the path goes off to the left to cut off a bend in the river and secondly if you go down to the river bank on the right, you will find a series of delightful waterfalls. As the path approaches the river again you will see a ruin over to the right, Lammerside Castle, keep your eye on it for the path goes past the front door. Continue straight ahead until you are level with the castle and then turn right through a gate and across the meadow, in front of the ruin. Next go through a gate and straight across the field to another gate. Pass through it and proceed straight ahead with a fence on the right to another gate, turning right through it and alongside the wall to yet another

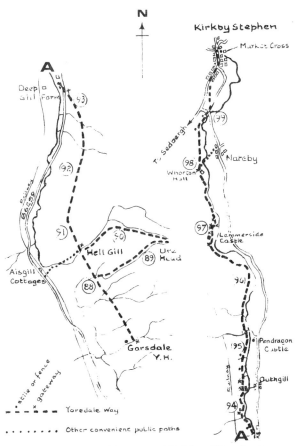

N

Kirkby Stephen

Market Cross

Deep
Gill Farm (93)

To Sedbergh

(99)

(92)

(98)

Nateby

Wharton
Hall

(91)

(90)

(97)

Lammerside
Castle

Hell Gill

(89) Ure
Head

(96)

Aisgill
Cottages

(88)

Railway

Pendragon
Castle

(95)

Garsdale
Y.H.

Outhgill

(94)

A

stile or fence
gateway

– – – Yoredale Way

. . . . Other convenient public paths

Garsdale Youth Hostel - Kirkby Stephen

65

gate on the left. Go through that gate and straight ahead to yet one more beyond which the path goes in the same direction to eventually join the access road to Wharton Hall at a cattle grid. Go along this track, past Wharton Hall and beyond a couple of silos you will have noticed as you came along from Lammerside. Proceed through a gate on the right and across the field to the wooded banks of the River Eden, turning left along the wall side. Unless you wish to go over to Nateby, where bed and breakfast and bar snacks are available, ignore the bridge on the right and continue along the river bank towards a hill. There is a fence which skirts round the right-hand side of the hill, follow this, keeping to the right of the fence to a ladder stile over a wall. The river at this point makes a delightful picture as it wends its way through the wooded banks and after passing through a gap between the wall and the trees where a gate used to bar the way, we get our first glimpse of our journey's end, the market town of Kirkby Stephen. Continue in the same direction to the corner of the field. Climb over a fence as the stile has disappeared and climb down some steps to a built-up path which goes under the old railway bridge and alongside the waterfall before some steps lead up to the road above. To get a better view of the waterfall, cross the road and about fifty yards to the left is a path which will take you down to the other side of the road bridge. The very last short section of the walk is reached about three hundred yards further down the road where a footpath sign on the left-hand side of the road points the way through a gate and a well-trodden path cuts diagonally across the fields and into Kirkby Stephen. The long journey is over, or perhaps it isn't, why not continue along the Eden to Carlisle, the Coast to Coast either to St. Bees or to Robin Hood's Bay or join the Pennine Way at Keld and tramp north or south as the spirit moves?

For those with a little initiative, there is the opportunity to join the Dales Way at Sedbergh and from there to continue along that fine walk to the shores of Lake Windermere or alternatively to take the opposite path to Ilkley and the Ebor Way route to return to York, a round journey of some two hundred miles.

Those who are so disposed should leave the path at Hell Gill, go down to Aisgill Moor cottages, crossing the road to join the bridleway which goes southward and then swings to the north-west over Turner Hill and along past High Flust to join the infant River Rawthey at Rawthey Foot. From this point there are public footpaths either beside or very near to the river all the way to Sedbergh.

The Reverse

The description of the walk in the preceding pages is from York to Kirkby Stephen only because this was the direction in which it was first walked. It is inevitable that it will be more convenient for some walkers to start at Kirkby Stephen and the following notes are provided to assist without confusing the main text. Whilst certainly not an adequate description of the reverse path, the notes should be of assistance if used in conjunction with the directions given in the preceding pages and the appropriate maps.

Kirkby Stephen to Hawes

From the market cross at Kirkby Stephen go southward past the turning on the left, signposted Nateby and on to a footpath sign on the left-hand side of the road and a path clearly defined across the meadows to the Nateby road. Turn right and approximately three hundred yards along the road at a sign 'Footpath to Wharton' turn right down some steps to the river. There are really no problems all the way to Wharton, the path keeps close to the river all the way. Past the Hall our path leaves the main track just beyond a cattle grid, veering left across the field and through two gates. After the second, turn right to another one and then left and through two more to Lemmerside Castle which you will have seen ahead. After you have passed the ruins go through another gate and turn left along a very good track which passes to the right of a hill and on to Pendragon Castle. Our route now lies along the road which goes down the hill to the left past some cottages on the right. Turn right through a gate on the right just before the river bridge and after passing over a stream, maintain the same direction over stiles and along a narrow walled track to Shoregill. Passing round the cottages and down the access road, continue along the riverside to the next farm and go up the road to the farm, and through the farmyard to a gate and continue along the riverside. Cross over a wall stile and then follow the path which goes over a bridge and winds up to the Kirkby Stephen road. Turn right along the road for a short distance to a gate on the left, passing through it and southward up a well defined track to Hell Gill Bridge, recognized quite easily by a gate leading on to a stone bridge spanning a deep ravine. The tiny River Ure is easily found when walking in this direction as it is the first stream crossed after passing Hell Gill.

As we continue over the Ure, our path goes straight ahead at approximately the same level with a wall on the right, past the Youth Hostel and on until a stone kiln is reached. Walk past the kiln, go through a small gate and swing left towards a hole in the wall. Go through the hole and down the hill between the forestry fence and the wall to the Cotterdale road, turning left along it into the hamlet. After the farms and cottages go straight ahead to a bridge over the stream, turning right over it, then through a gate and up the forestry track. At the top pass through a gate and turn right along the edge of the forestry to a very good track which takes you round the edge of Great Shunner to join the Pennine Way at the point where it comes down from the left past some cairns. Our route now follows the Pennine Way, turning right through a gate and down a walled track into Hardrow.

Follow the path now past the church and over a stream to a narrow lane to the right and a clear track, well trampled by Pennine Way walkers to Hawes.

Hawes to West Witton
From Hawes it is necessary to retrace one's steps over the river bridge, past the cricket ground and then through a stile on the right and across the field at an angle to a tiny bridge over a stream. Maintain the same direction through a stile, across the road and a further series of stiles to Sedbusk.

Turn left toward the hamlet, but take the farm access road on the right and after passing through a gate keep straight ahead towards some farms and a gated track which is clearly defined all the way to Skellgill. Turn right over the tiny packhorse bridge and along the metalled track for one mile. Immediately after a sharp right bend, turn left through a gate and along a good clear path to Mill Gill waterfall. The path is then clearly marked into Askrigg.

From the church go straight across the road, turn right and go down a lane between two houses which eventually leads into a walled grassy track. Go down the lane and straight ahead through stiles, across a road and down a lane to Nappa House. At a right angle bend, just before the house, a footpath sign beside a stile indicates the route ahead along the northern side of the railway formation. There is an old iron bridge with stone buttresses ahead and about two hundred yards beyond it a kissing gate on the southern side of the formation which takes a bit of finding among the hawthorn bushes. Go through the gate and turn left along the side of the hedge and then through stiles beside the river to a footbridge. Turn left up a track for a very short distance before passing over a stile on the right and cutting across the field toward the buttresses of a demolished railway bridge. Go between them and then veer right across the field to a stile and beyond that another one. After the second one veer right across the field to yet one more stile and a further series of stiles beyond, which lead one to a farm gate and beyond the old railway formation yet again. Go over it through a gate, turning left with a hedge on the left along a pleasant path which passes the Upper Falls at Aysgarth and the river bridge beyond.

Turn right over the river bridge, past the mill and up through a gate into the churchyard, passing through it and along a lane to the main road beyond. Cross the road to a stile and straight ahead to another one in Thieves Gill, walking almost due south through a series of stiles to the West Burton road. Turn right along the road and over a bridge, go through a stile on the right, then across a field to a gate and continue in the same direction to a bend in the beck. Climb through two stiles very close together and then the path turns left over a field, passing to the right of a barn and straight into West Burton.

The route from West Burton starts at the tiny packhorse bridge and needs very little description. Three miles along this wonderful drove road you will see a caravan site down to the left and shortly after a derelict barn up to the right. Just before this you will find a stile on the left through which is the path down through the wood at the bottom of the hill and into West Witton. For those wishing to climb Pen Hill, the directions are as in the first part of the book.

West Witton to Masham
On the left-hand side of the road at the east end of West Witton village there is a stile which leads to another stile and then into a narrow walled lane which is easy to follow. Continue along to a gate with a stile beside it, pass over the stile and keeping a wall on the left, go up the hill away from the wall. At the top of the hill is a track going down the other side, follow this to a series of stiles, crossing a narrow track and along the riverside walk to Wensley.

Turn left over the river bridge and then left through the main gates of Bolton Hall, continuing along the concrete track to a gate on the right which gives access to open parkland. Go diagonally right and up the hill to a small cottage passing to the right of it. Proceed through a gate and immediately through another gate on the left and across a field to yet an additional one. Go through that gate, then along a short length of path through the trees and turn right along a wide track to the road. Turn left along the road to a footpath sign and a stile on the right which will guide you over a meadow, across the railway, through another meadow and over a road to the access road to Tullis Cote Farm. Beyond the farm turn right alongside the farm buildings and walk through the gates and along a narrow wood. At the end of the wood turn left through a gate, go straight across a field and turn right up a track which will take you up on to the Shawl and a straight walk into Leyburn.

On the right-hand side of the road just beyond the east end of the market place and opposite the church, go down a narrow lane over a railway bridge and past some bungalows on the left. Keep straight ahead with farms on the left down through stiles to a gate immediately before a farm which can be seen ahead. Proceed through the gate or the stile beside it, keep straight ahead, past farm buildings on the right to the road, and turning right along it, go over the river bridge and into Middleham.

From Middleham go down the track to the left of the castle, turning left after passing through a gate. Go over the hill, then through a gate and straight ahead to a wood and the banks of the River Cover. Next turn left along the river bank to the **Cover Bridge Inn.** Over the river bridge turn left through a small gate and walk along the river bank on a good path to a point where a wide track goes up to the road and Jervaulx Abbey is up the hill to the left.

Go through the gate towards the abbey, following the track which goes to the right of it through the parkland, past a pond and out onto a minor road. Turn left along the road for approximately one mile, turning right through a gate just before a farm and wander along a clear track across the field to the river. After a gate with part of a railway coupling for a fastening, keep to the right with a hedge on the right eventually to join a cart track which swings right into Low Ellington.

Continue past the farm on the left and along the road for about two hundred yards to a stile in the wall on the left. Cross over the stile and go straight ahead along a track which swings left round a hill to join a good track. It then passes through a gate and then goes left to High Mains Farm. Go through the gate beside the farmhouse and to the right of the farm buildings and through two more gates to swing right and along the path to the riverside. The path now continues close to the river for most of the way and will not present any problems all the way to Masham.

Masham to Boroughbridge

From the market place at Masham go into the churchyard, turning right past the ancient shaft on the left and straight ahead to a gate. Turn right along the edge of the field to join a wide track, turning left along it, past a black hut. Veer right across a field to a stile and then left along a minor road. Over the river bridge turn left through a gate and continue along the river bank, going up to the right to join a farm track just beyond a farm. Turn left along this track and then left along the side of a field with a wood on the left. Continue along the fence to some gorse bushes, pass through a gate beyond them and turn left down a track which swings right and then along the riverside to Mickley.

Turn left along the lane at the end of the village and right over a stile after the last cottage. Keep straight ahead to a stile and beyond it turn left along the side of a wood and an easy to follow path. Go through another small wood and straight ahead to yet another delightful walk along the riverside path. Emerging from the woods at a bend in the river, there is a farm straight ahead, turn right with a wall on the right, continue through a small gate and along to the far side of the field. Turn left along the hedge to a wide track and turn right along it to West Tanfield.

West Tanfield to Slenningford Grange is no problem; keep to the path along the south bank of the river to the caravan park and then to the high level path with a fence on the left to the Grange. Go over the stile near some buildings, but do not go through the gate straight ahead, instead turn left with a fence on the right for about thirty yards and then go downhill left over a stile. After the stile turn right, round the end of a copse, through an iron gate and up a green track to the main road. Turn left along it into North Stainley.

Just before the church turn left along a track which passes to the right of the cricket ground. After you have passed a nature reserve, veer right through a gate and across a field to some cottages, then pass through a gate to the right of them. Keep straight on along the track which goes straight to Middle Parks Farm, turning right after passing through a gate. Follow this on past a lake to a junction where our path lies to the left to High Parks Farm. Through the farmyard and two gates beyond, turn right past the front of a bungalow, go through a further gate and then cut across the field diagonally left, (Ripon Cathedral should be visible directly ahead). Next walk down a path through a small wood, turning right along the riverside path to Ripon.

The route through Ripon presents no problems, just keep straight ahead past the cathedral and turn left at the roundabout, taking the path alongside the old canal. Keep left of the canal along the towpath which passes between the canal and the racecourse, crossing over the canal at a humpback bridge and then along the other side to Ox Close Locks. Continue along the river bank past Newby Hall and over stiles and small bridges to Roecliffe where the path goes up the hill. Follow it through a stile and alongside the church into the village.

Turn left along the road out of the village and then turn right along a lane which turns left before passing over the old railway formation and is very easy to follow to the road. Turn right along the road, under the A1 and go through the gate on the left immediately opposite the Devil's Arrows and along a good track into Boroughbridge.

Boroughbridge to York

Leaving Boroughbridge, go past the **Three Horse Shoes,** then over the river bridge and turn right through a gate and along the river bank. Follow the path over the lock, turn right and continue along the riverside to Ellenthorpe Hall where just after the Hall and farm buildings, you will find a gate on the left. Pass through it and turn right along the access road to Ellenthorpe Lodge. Go through the farm buildings and straight ahead past some greenhouses on the left to a bridge over a stream. Veer right across Myton Meadows after crossing the bridge and pass over the bridge spanning the River Swale, turning left into Myton village. After passing through the village, take the first turn right down a metalled track which eventually changes into a rough bridletrack which leads to Aldwark village.

At the far end of the village, just opposite the church go towards the farm, swinging right and through a gate, and following a tractor track which swings left away from Aldwark Manor and continues through two more gates and across a field to the corner of a wood. Turn right with the wood on the left, following a green track which swings right away from the wood and joins a clear track down to the road on the right. Turn left along the road for a mile and then right along a track just past Youlton Hall. Continue along this track which eventually changes to a road and then on past farms on the left to a sharp right bend with a farm on the corner. Go through the farmyard to the right of the farmhouse and straight ahead along a green way to a tiny bridge over the River Kyle. Turn right and continue a little distance from the river, going down to a stile at the river's edge and then to a couple of gates to emerge into the village of Newton-on-Ouse.

Turn left into the village of Newton, pass the church and some bungalows before turning right over a stile and down to the river. Finally turn left along the bank to Beningbrough and on to York.